Baby On The Water

New and Selected Poems

Tsaurah Litzky

Long Shot Productions

Hoboken, NJ

First Edition
9 8 7 6 5 4 3 2
Printed in the United States of America

Cover art and interior art by Carri Skoczek
Back cover photo by Joel Litzky
Cover design by Elizabeth van Itallie
Layout by Michael C. Cote

Some of these poems have appeared in *Long Shot, The Outlaw Bible of* ·
American Poetry, Appearances, Allspice, Downtown, Stories from the Infir-
mary, Pink Pages, Best American Erotica 1995, Café Review, Unbearables, In
Your Face, Hart – A Journal of Poetry, Poetry Magazine of the Lower East
Side, Pushing Out the Envelope, The Blue Bird Buddha of No Regrets, Prayer
to the Ultimate Cosmic Satellite Dish, Blessing Poems, Kamikaze Lover, Good
Bye Beautiful Mother.

Thank you, Thank you, Thank you, – Danny Shot, Tomassso, Lynn
Ossa, Ron Kolm, Robert Polito, Jackson Taylor, Carri Skoczek, John
Davis, Susie Bright, Hersch Silverman, Margo Free, and my family,
especially Joel

Library of Congress Cataloging-in-Publication Data
Litzky, Tsaurah
    Baby on the Water/Tsaurah Litzky. – 1st ed.
        p. cm.
    ISBN 0-9654738-7-2 (alk. paper)
    I. Title
    PS3612.I898B33 2003
    811'.6--dc21   2003040126

Long Shot Productions
P.O. Box 6238
Hoboken, NJ 07030

www.longshot.org

Contents

Pushing Out the Envelope

Blessings

Good Bye Beautiful Mother

Why do Yoga?

Dedicated to the ratty garters that hold up the loopy edges of impossible desire.

Pushing
Out the
Envelope

Snake Dream

I dreamed my mother became a two headed snake,
her ivory skin grown scaly and emerald.
Two identical forked tongues flicked in and out
of her lipless mouths, she was telling me something,
hissing and snapping.
Only her eyes were unchanged, but multiplied by two,
huge, brown, as shiny and wet with tears as always
when she wanted to win me over.

I woke up, I remembered Lucy Benedetto telling me,
when her mother was dying of cancer,
the mother started to talk in tongues.
I knew the snake was the God of Death,
so I picked up the phone and dialed,
My mother got it on the second ring,
"Hello," and more sharply, "Hell-oo?"
she sounded fine, and then,
"Meshuganehs, crazies, five o'clock in the morning,"
she said, slamming the receiver down.

Years after I left home,
she asked why, why so many men,
"Just because I am not married," I answered,
"Does that mean I should be penalized,
does that mean I shouldn't have a sex life?"
"But so many?" my mother said.

Now I am a performance artist,
no time for chasing my tail,
I do Yoga and assume the Cobra position,
it combats menstrual pain.
I do the Breath of Fire and stand on my head,
I don't spread my legs.

My mother tells her friends I'm in show biz.

The Shower

The new shower is so white and clean I think I am in a motel.
It was put in two days ago by an artist carpenter, Cliff
    Gerstenhaber.
The new landlord hired him. Gerstenhaber was cute, so I said
    smiling, "What kind of name is Gerstenhaber?"
"A long name," he said, not smiling.
You win some you lose some, I thought.

It took Gerstenhaber one day to do the job,
the old shower was put in by my old boyfriend, Louis Krim.
It took Louis two weeks to put it in.
The first time I used that shower it leaked on Bob and Betty
    downstairs.
Bob doesn't like me because he once made a play for me
and I squashed him.
Betty doesn't like me because she knows something happened,
but not what.
They think I am promiscuous and will never amount to anything,
they are wrong on both counts.
The old landlord would not put out any more money to fix
the shower, he said he had fulfilled his obligations.
They said I should shower in the public bathroom on the second
    floor.

I said I was paying for the shower and would use the shower,
they should fight the landlord.
One time when I was in the shower with Abraham, the shower
leaked so much they called 911. They said maybe someone was
having a heart attack in the shower.
The police broke the door down with an axe, ha, ha, ha.

I take a lot of showers, my mother told me it was an ancient Jewish
beauty secret and she was so beautiful, although I wondered where
the ancient Jews took showers when they wandered around
in the desert with Moses.

Yesterday I took a shower and the shower doesn't leak.
Time magazine says the freedom the future promises women
can be frightening, but the effect of feminism has been positive.
Today Betty said, "Hi ya, how ya doing?" when we passed in the hall.

The Love Poem

I love boytoys in bustiers and fishnets,
hedging my bets, no regrets, nynoxyl nine, two at a time,
red meat, back streets, dirty sheets and light spankings,
and if I were a teapot I could blow off some of this steam,
in a former life I must have been a CIA agent or a cocktease queen,
I'm so hungry for love, hungry for love, hungry for love,
I love every man who likes me.
I used to go to bed with men who bought me a cup of coffee,
I switched to tea,
I was into the ecstasy of variety, yoni piety,
but I couldn't stay cool, they threw me out of refrigerator school,
because whenever I wanted a man I blew a fuse.
I practiced unconditional love, but every time I had good sex
with a man I wanted him to stay with me forever and
I could not help telling him that, so I had good sex one time
with many, many men.
Now I'm trying to educate myself so I read mystery stories
because in mystery stories justice prevails, and
I haven't got a clue why the only three women
I met in the last year who I trust are lesbians,
or why my capacity for multiple orgasms increases if I
keep on my shoes, and I'm learning to tell jokes
like anyone can become president,
the country is pulling out of the recession,
or men respect women more now because of feminism.
I know animal terror when I see it and I see it a lot
when I write "I love sex" on my forehead.
I love the sight of a man walking down the street
carrying flowers, especially when I gave him those flowers,
but why I keep falling for men who are allergic to flowers
is a mystery to me.
This started out as a love poem,
but I made so many mistakes in love
that I feel qualified to take responsibility for my choices,
to tattoo "Take no prisoners" on my labia,
to apply for a miracle,
to do it with the goat god on the highest mountain,
to die while I'm doing it under the full moon,
to go to Kundalini Corner in Buddha Heaven,
to go there soon.

Pushing Out the Envelope

I heard it on the TV, breast augmentation is the most popular
    plastic surgery.
You could say a lot of people are concerned with pushing out the
    envelope.
I thought pushing out the envelope meant exceeding your
    boundaries figuratively,
but how much more literal can you get then a silicon inset.

My lover didn't like my breasts,
he did me best if I put on the bustier I wore the first time we met,
since he left, I've been pushing out the envelope,
losing my third eye in a get rich quick scheme,
drinking twenty cups of coffee a day with sugar and cream,
pushing out the envelope, pushing out the envelope
because nothing is as it seems.
I take a hundred vitamin E pills and do yoga for three hours,
I want to communicate with the higher powers.
I masturbate till I hyphenate and kill the parakeet as a
sacrifice to Billy Holiday,
I'll do anything to push the envelope out except plastic surgery,
hard drugs or armed robbery,
particularly since I can't shoot straight,
and I have to face the truth about myself,
there are men who can make me forget my hard won
self respect quicker than you can say blowjob,
and I want to face the truth about myself,
I can't control my needs anymore than I can fill them,
but who really cares about the extent of my masochism
except I hear, it's universal, ask any bartender;
there are more tears shed in bars than there are stars,
if we could harness pain we could turn the desert green,
carbonate Boston Harbor, mend the ozone layer, save the whales,
and since true love is such a washout,
I'm working from the inside trying to push the envelope out.

My lover sent me a postcard saying he was killed
in an avalanche, buried under a mountain of breasts.
Now I'm getting ready for what comes next,
driving 115 m.p.h. in a toy car,
dressing up as the Pope and going to a transvestite bar,
dancing the cha-cha-cha on the Brooklyn Bridge at 4 a.m.
looking for a solution without a problem,
I bind my breasts with rawhide and send Santa Claus
a letter looking for a mail order bride and
I'm pushing out the envelope, pushing out the envelope,
because I want the world to climb inside.

Neo-Anarcho Feminist Manifesto for the Twenty-First Century

Don't give him blow jobs if he won't go down on you,
stop nursing every man who calls you mama,
carry your own condoms, make sure they are extra-sensitive,
    extra-thin,
stop nursing every man who calls you baby,
never wear charm bracelets or floral prints,
sleep with the men you want,
sleep with the women you want,
don't put down other women,
don't put down who they choose to sleep with.
Pay for your own drinks,
unless you drink Margaritas.
I drink Margaritas.

Don't be anyone's band aid and don't share your K-Y jelly,
discretion is the better part of fidelity,
particulary if you don't like to sleep alone,
men have always known this.
Don't ever ask a man,
Did you miss me, do you love me,
do you want me, do you need me?
Ask him if he likes jelly roll and knows how to iron.

Prayer

Buddha of Suppressed Desires,
Buddha of lonely women who wait by the phone,
of nut fudge decadence and tacky, overpriced designer clothes,
stop me from punishing myself to justify rejection,
from making myself grotesque,
False Plastic Geisha Buddha of Collegen Complexion Masks and
    Electrolysis,
do not tempt me with dermabrasion
or acupuncture face lifts,
Blindspot Buddha of Dimly Lit Bars,
stop me from making a fool of myself
over much younger men,
save me from buying them dinner and getting their drugs,
save me from my old has-been wannabe dreams,
and the patronizing dogma of feminism when
it is based on motherhood rather than personhood.

Cock-Eyed-Owl Buddha of the Broken Alarm Clock,
Unanswered Letter, Lost Keys, Vanished Friends,
return, restore my lost opportunities, bring me new ones.
Introduce me to your baby, the Blue Bird Buddha of No Regrets,
infinite options, exciting conversations.
Buccaneer Buddha of Broadway,
Buddha with Cowboy Boots On, Buddha of the Crapshoot,
Buddha of the Luck of the Draw, watch over me as I
prowl though futuristic cyber punk cities of recycled poetry
looking for an android fuck machine
with the soul of a musician,
come, sit beside me in ubiquitous, shoddy Greek luncheonettes
where I wait for the Dionysus of feta cheese and grape leaves.

Best Blessed Budhha of the Coffee Grinder and Multiple Orgasms,
teach me to accept my life, to open into it without fear,
Oh, bright Boddhisattva, brilliant, blackberry,
blue eagle, bobcat, boogie-woogie boomerang,
bouncing boundless Smith Corona Buddha of my typewriter,
help me.

Late Night Liquor Delivery

Forty-nine years old and what the hell,
black river, no moon,
cat got my tongue
and swallowed it.

Untitled

Why am I so cruel to myself, my typewriter,
space bar cracked, keys gone undusted…

Dead Louis

—for Louis Cartwright

No more rhumba,
no bright blue robin's egg,
no abbracadabra.

In the Country of Pinched Nerves

— for Nathan Versace

I thirsted for a heroic life,
instead I am the Queen of dead lasagna,
obscene 3 A.M. phone calls,
bottom of the bottle vendettas and
hairy eyeballs,

glue mousetraps and liposuction are
my gifts to the world,

Oh, I am the Queen of messy potties,
bumpy nipples and soiled panties,
empires of lipstick can not disguise
my grim and abysmal face,
enigmatic as the black holes in space,
because I am the Queen of self pity,
split zippers, dirty ears, mad, howling rabid dogs,
tse-tse flies, golliwogs and electric chairs,

the regal, purple corridors of my mind
erupt into evil fiefdoms of delusive expectations,
I am the Queen of interrupted masturbation,

in all my dominions there are no graceful ballerinas,
no love at first sight,
and I stand here before you tonight,
in my crown of pinched nerves,
to issue this royal proclamation:
Time is disgrace without a theme
and night is about falling,
because I am the Queen, the Queen of dead lasagna,
I am the Queen…

Cursing Shiva

Shiva, your blood is rot gut wine,
thunderbird and turpentine,

Shiva, Mahaveda, God of Cosmic Dissolution,
apocrypha, anathema, gruesome goon,
as dangerous as a million gone Godzillas,
global anarchy in hamstring pants,
slimy, slinky, stinky sex salamander,
Lord of the Cosmic Dance,

scofflaw in the eye of true love,
steel fingers in the boxing glove,
Shiva with your cheap cigars,
you give bad haircuts, broken eyelids,
greasy teeth, cement donuts,
rancid lysergic acid and crows feet,

you're the one leap of faith this poor bitch can not make,
you're my one botched abortion, two ex-husbands,
three dead junkie friends stomach ache,

sometimes you turn me into a thrashing, grasping fish,
fawning after tentative invitations,
Shiva, spear carrier of everlasting agitation,
or you send me to art openings in Soho
with too much lipstick on,
demonic bozo, narcissistic mastodon,
nihilistic Shiva of the black heart, broken date,
false start, premature ejaculate,

you rat-tail Attila, cobra mahatma, urine enema,
Shiva, Shiva arch deceiver,
shyster, sucker, trickster, monster,
eternally fanning the candles of darkness,
dancing the jig on the holy beds of aids martyrs,
Shiva, Shiva, contra dharma false alarmer,
with your glance of flaming spiders
that makes everything dissolve,
damm you, damm you, damm you.

For Jack Micheline

Poet laureate of the cracked seashell,
Poet laureate of the wacked out, crippled seagull,
Emperor of oceans of jangled emotions,
you never run out of french fries,

you picked up a piece of beach glass
and on Coney Island sands you scratched,
Every time I get out of my skin, I die.

Oh, conqueror of Cyclone's highest spire,
poised on a pinnacle of blue-est sky,
then soaring out over the briny keep,
then diving deep into nightmare sleep
to catch a pearly poem in your teeth,

Jack Micheline,
Poet Laureate of the cracked seashell,
gardener, gleaner, reaper, keeper, mindsweeper,

Guardian of the Golden Bell.

Rhapsody in Womb

—for Ursula Clark

the womb is stronger than the passions of assholes,
the womb is radiant beyond belief,
the womb contains the treasues of every lost paradise,
the womb is a room with no windows and plenty of heat.

the womb is the only holy fig, it comes without a trigger,
it unifies desire, give relevance to pain,
it's the golden fleece, the Rosetta stone,
the holy grail, the only free cocaine,
the womb does not own a Harley or a cock ring,
the womb does not take anti-histamines,
the womb comes in every shade of tangerine,
coral, orange, ruby, orchid, and the womb is always green.

the womb has regular bowel movements,
it does not own a winter hat, it has no feet,
but it can take a man and make him dance,
it can twirl him, whirl him, swirl him, curl him,
tickle his balls with peacock feathers or steel cleats,
the womb smells of scorched hair, shoe trees,
dried blood and poison ink,
the womb stinks.
the womb is kosher and does not suffer from claustrophobia,
only the womb can conquer corporate America,
it holds the blueprint for every parallel universe,
the womb is silent on the transmigration of souls,
the womb never wears nylons,
the womb proves anything can happen
from Mother Theresa to Charlie Manson.

anyone can have a womb
because a womb is a mind
and the one true eternal womb
is in the mind of every life,
age can not wither it away.

sometimes the womb is a bitch,
the witches hold their sabbath in the womb,
but it's always Wigstock in the womb,
they serve the best whiskey in the womb,
they're exploding roman candles in the womb,
BOOM, BOOM, BOOM, BOOM,
let's hear it for the womb, three cheers for the womb,
HOORAY, HOORAY, HOORAY!

Valediction

forsaking the gentle laxatives of
water and yoga,
I drink two cups of coffee
with sugar and milk,
I get quick results,
rise, excrete,
salute the sixteen inch stool in the bowl,
try to identify the bones
of two pieces of pizza, one jelly donut,
six oreos.

Being and nothingness is an uphill road.

Pressured Poets Pantoum

I can only do one thing at a time and I have so many things to do,
pressure, like a screw whose threads meet in a single, sharp point,
is driving me deeper and deeper underground. I want to move
to an opium den in Jakarta where the moon is midnight blue.

Pressure, like a screw whose threads meet in a single, sharp point,
is boring holes in my defenses, holes for fears to slip through,
to an opium den in Jakarta where the moon is midnight blue,
I want my dragons to float sedated up among the starry plumes.

Is making holes in my defenses, holes for fear to slip through
the work of the dancing devils of Dakar, the devils in pantaloons?
I want my dragons to float sedated up among the starry plumes
while my desires are soothed by the silver tongues of sitars and oods.

The work of the Dancing Devils of Dakar, the devils in pantaloons,
is to use my bones for candlesticks and to burn my eyes for
	candlewicks
while my desires are soothed by the silver tongues of sitars and oods;
Blinded, shamed, I try to hide my gouged face among the veiled
	women,
I can only do one thing at a time and I have so many things to do.

How I Got my Apartment

He was uncircumcised and he showed me how to pull back the little cowl and clean the mucousy stuff off with a washcloth. I could count the knots climbing up his spine; my private rosary, my prayer of pale flesh. I first saw him at the Easter Be-In. I had a yellow flower painted on my face. He was carrying a sketch pad and wearing a red and black plaid wool jacket. I didn't know then that red and black were the colors to wear on a vision quest. I was making my way through gone girls in granny skirts and would-be Maharishis in tie-dyed vests when I saw him and he saw me. We stopped and smiled at each other, standing about three feet apart, transfixed. He was so beautiful I thought he might be a mirage or some enchanted mannequin fallen from the clouds. When I blinked he was gone.

Two days later he was there when I dropped in on some friends. That was when I knew there are no accidents. He asked me to go home with him. We walked over the Brooklyn Bridge to this building with a view of the Statue of Liberty from all the side windows. In the morning he reached his long arm over to the easel beside the bed, picked up a paint brush and drew a line down the center of my head forever changing the part of my hair. He said he wanted to show me the desert and asked me to go to New Mexico with him.

I quit my job. We bought a truck at a Con Edison auction. At night he held me and told me about the Sangre De Cristo Mountains, where breathing the air makes you high. He was my Jesus, my blue eyes, my boat across the Sea of Galilee. He taught me how to roll tobacco or reefer so I could roll while he drove. You make two little piles of flake inside the folded paper so the flake looks like a couple of mice swallowed by a snake, then you squash the little mice with your index finger and thumbs and roll the paper into a tight cylinder. We scored in Pittsburgh, Columbus, Chicago and St. Louis. We slept in truck stops. In the morning he would draw me naked and rosy lying on our piles of clothes. Out in the parking lot, truckers would walk by joking, high on amphetamines and coffee. Before we left New York he bought me a low cut peasant blouse with blue flowers embroidered on it. I made good use of it.

All the way across Route 66 we looked for groceries and convenience stores with a man on duty behind the register. I would select a token loaf of bread, stuff the pockets of my loose denim skirt with cheese, lunch meats, little red boxes of raisins and go up to the check-out counter. Then I would pull my peasant blouse down between my breasts and smile.

In Santa Fe he wanted to leave me, said I was too emotional, talked to strangers about my feelings, wasn't cool. Then he sold a few drawings, decided to stay, made me sandals and a hashish pipe from the thigh bone of a chicken. At the peyote rituals I waited with the Indian women outside the sweat lodge and when he stepped out I handed him an ear of roasted corn. We met the Pranksters, got on the bus, Babs said I was good looking, Kesey traded him a sketch for a book, Gary Snyder's *Rip Rap Poems*.

We lit out for the coast. I panhandled in Golden Gate Park while he sat drawing in the back of the truck. We got a job rolling marijuana cigarettes in chocolate papers for a wizard who sold them by the pack from a houseboat in Sausalito. We crashed with friends of his in the Mission.

I scavenged for our dinners in the dumpsters outside the Grand Union where I met other stoned gleaners, gatherers for their tribes. He got a job as a shipping clerk, spent the money on rent and art supplies. He shaved off all my pubic hair, then all his pubic hair, and we fucked as innocents. We were happy. When the hair started to grow back, he shaved us again. Then he lost his job; I was too spaced out to look for a job. We couldn't help his friends with the rent anymore so we hit the road. We drove south to L.A. where his German mother told me Jewish parents spoil their children, coddle them. I told her how I crawled through mountains of garbage to find a pack of stale English muffins to feed her son while he was sitting in his friend's kitchen drawing pictures of rainbows.

Back on the road we quarreled. I said he had his drawing, his art. I wanted something of my own, a home, a baby. He said maybe later, when he was established, had a studio. I said, "Why does it always have to be what you want?" We drove back to New York and returned to this, his old building. We stayed with George on the second floor. My hair was down to the cleft in my ass and I got a job at Max's. I spent my tip money on groceries and cooked us vegetarian dinners. During the day he went foraging for reefer and acid. I was a lousy waitress, no one seemed to notice. He wasn't drawing, he said he missed the desert.

One day he asked me if I had ever cheated on him. I don't know why, but I made up a long lie about how I met a guy named Brian when I was scavenging in the dumpsters. This mythical Brian took me to a black room, lit incense and candles and then drew flowers with cocaine on my thighs. The story I told him was that I had gone to visit Brian in the black room several times.

He slapped me so hard my jaw popped. "Brian must have loved you," he said. When I came home from work at four A.M. the next day, he and the truck were gone.

Later I found out he had gone across the street to the garage where John the sculptor lived, given him a blow job and borrowed 200 dollars. The next day, Franklin, the guy who lived on the top floor here, told me he was moving to Germany to be with his lover Axel. He sold me this apartment with everything in it, for seventy-five dollars. I still don't know why I told that lie, maybe because I know there are no accidents.

Vision Quest

I used to consult the I Ching all the time. Should I call him, should I not call him? *Perseverance furthers* or *hasty action would not be wise*, the book replied. The pages of my old journals are covered with those scratchy hexagrams, marks of my unquiet soul. Crouched in my room, throwing pennies on the floor, I asked the same questions again and again, buying time, biding time until my anger passed because my rage at the unfairness of life was so great I could kill. I was learning that there is no way you can make anyone love you and also that there are people who will love you no matter what you do. I brought my ex-husband to the house I shared with Peter and screwed him in our bed.

Then I told Peter about it. His only comment was, "I guess you had to get him out of your system." *Gradual Development*, the I Ching said that day, *Progress*. I grew tired of the I Ching, Astrology, Tarot, all the gods of hocus-pocus, mumbo-jumbo, realized my friend Jayne the Astrologer was the unhappiest person I ever had the sad fortune to know. When friends said they had to use the I Ching or throw the Runes, I heard myself say, "Can't you think for yourself?" One day I tossed my I Ching in the garbage, put on my magic red beret and went out into the street on a vision quest. The first thing I saw was a woman giving a man a blow job in a yellow Datsun Sentra.

I took up Yoga, learned to stand on my head, arch my back like a cat, coil like a cobra. The Yogis say the body is a wishing stone. I found I could climb over mountains of anger doing breath of fire while seated in the lotus pose, but it was not enough. I used the credit card my parents gave me for emergencies to hop a plane for Barbados and when a washed-out old hippie soldier of fortune asked me to drop acid with him, I said yes. We sailed his boat to St. Thomas and there, in the Jewish cemetery at midnight, had intercourse on the grave of Isabella Mariano Mendes, beloved daughter, mother, wife. He wanted to add me to his stable of three women but I ran away, escaped with my life.

Back in New York, I have a miscarriage, drink coffee till my eyeballs sweat, start to write. My narcissism disgusts me and keeps me going at the same time. I read my poetry at Opens and learn that I am not the only one playing with a deck that has too many cards. I fall for a man who says he will give me a baby. He gets cold feet, says we are both too unstable, gives me an African violet instead. When I crush its leaves between my fingers, it bleeds a clear sap that smells like fresh cut grass. I stay up all night trying to make the black shadows around me fade to purple. When people ask my astrological sign I lie and say I am a Scorpio if I want to appear sensual and exotic, or a Libra if I want to be considered socially adept and well balanced. This little ruse works very well but I am scared at how easily people accept these astrological categories as if the position of the stars was what it took to justify cruelty, avarice, the failures of love. I tell guys in bars that I am looking for a man with a heart in Aquarius, penis rising. They laugh, take a sip of beer, look around the bar for another woman to talk to.

Magazines begin to publish my poetry and I am invited to give readings. I have an affair with a bass player sixteen years younger than me. It starts out a lark but the sex between us is so astounding I want to die with him. I know I'm out of control. I've stepped into a hole and am falling but that does not stop me from baking him lasagnas, buying him silver jewelry. He is frightened of my intensity, does not want an aging wife, flees to New Mexico as many have done before him. I have hot flashes, wet the bed at night while dreaming I am crawling through a dark tunnel towards a white light.

Then I meet a college writing instructor, gorgeous, blue eyes, chest like a stag, quite the catch. He has problems sustaining an erection and tells me it is my fault because I am a masochist and want to be hurt. Once I would have believed him but now I throw him out... *gradual development, progress...* I no longer own an I Ching but if I did I wonder what it would say; *The Arousing, shock, thunder* or *Waiting, nourishment,* or maybe, *work on what has been spoiled, decay.*

Christmas

This Christmas I want a miracle. I want to purge myself of cynicism and despair. I want to walk on water, grow the wings of an angel, learn to sing on key, and always be joyful in the company of friends. I don't want a little plaster creche with a tiny plaster baby Jesus or a plastic tree, I want peace on Earth and the Star of Bethlehem. My mother told me Jesus was not the son of God because if he were the son of God and had walked on the earth the Holocust could not have happened. She said we were still waiting for the Savior. If I kept looking out the window, I might see him coming up the street on the shoulders of F.D.R. and my dead grandpa Max. However, I was not so easily appeased. I wanted Christmas and a larger, more mysterious world than the one she defended with her vacuum cleaner and old wives tales.

I wanted the wine and the wafer, the blood and the body, and everything else I did not know, so I started to hang out with the Irish boys from Gerritson Beach.

One Christmas night I went with Dennis Keith Patrick O'Reilly into the back seat of his father's parked Plymouth Fury and showed him my rosy new breasts. He made me come with his fingers; then I rubbed the hard bulge under his black chinos until it flattened and grew moist beneath my hand. Suddenly he turned from me, sat up, crossed himself, and said, "Mea culpa, mea culpa, mea maxima culpa." I asked him what that meant, but he would not tell me. Later I found out it meant he was ashamed.

I could not understand this puzzling connection between pleasure and shame. I tried wilder Gerritson beach boys, crazy ones, drag racers, arsonists, but they were so ashamed of themselves they had to carve their initials on their forearms with razor blades to remember their names. I always knew who I was, a would-be adventurer, a midget Rockette with more imagination than legs, trying to kick the moon. I grew muscles on both sides of my tongue and learned to give phenomenal blow jobs so I would always be the one in control.

Eventually, I found out I didn't like being in control - it was too much responsibility. I wanted to be the baby, the one who was taken care of. I also wanted a baby so I could control it, but I was too selfish to give over my body so another soul could grow. I wanted to escape my skin and find salvation in the Christian world, but I could not accept the idea of original sin or feel ashamed of how I prayed in the garden of my body.

My sex was the only thing about myself I could trust. I married a long-haired, hippie desperado who turned out to be a mama's boy. I left him and married him in different forms again and again. Finally I learned I would not find Deus Ex Machina in the arms of mortal men, but I still want Christmas and virgin births and peace on Earth because I want to believe that bread is holy and God is love.

My neighbor Mary says I should get a dog. I tell her they are too needy and often have bad breath. I am lonely, going through menopause, too old to have a baby and now I regret my barrenness. At night I pile my bed with books and pour through them until my eyes are red looking for instructions on how to accept the fact that I am already an extinct species. Is the message of Christmas that the only hope is in acceptance? Kafka says no. Bukowski says yes, have some eggnogg, spread your legs.

My brother sent me a computer for Christmas but I have not yet unpacked it because it terrifies me. I went to hear a brilliant, young philosopher lecture on artificial intelligence. He said computers are more logical than people, and that being able to understand the essence of a zebra, as computers do, is more important than actually being able to see a zebra. Being able to understand the essence of another life would truly be a miracle for me. I can't understand my own life. Is being able to understand the essence of another life what love is? Maybe I should get a zebra and see, better yet, become a bone marrow doner or give a kidney or a rib and in that way survive in the body of another after the end of this, my illogical, biological life. Then I would be a holy ghost indeed.

In the Sacred and Profane Country of the Flesh

In the sacred and profane country of the flesh the body does not lie. There is mercy in the body and there are warnings: Danger, Thin Ice, Beware! When I ran across the kitchen to embrace you on your birthday, you patted me stiffly on the shoulder and I knew that she had won and the horror of it, I gave her the ammunition, I told her that you cross-dressed, I didn't know her well then, I didn't know what she was looking for, I should have picked up on it when she spoke of her Scottish lover Ryan, when she said you haven't made love until you've made love to a man in a kilt, I should have known right there it was you she was after. Her generous favors to me, her flattery, were all strategies in her campaign, and even if I prove to you that she manipulated me, even if I take you through it step by step, I know it will not make any difference to you now, you are her slave, her willing captive, with her tongue she has chained you, with her sex she has tied you down, she has told you she is in your shoes, she has promised you protection, there is nothing I can do and it's all so boring anyhow, it's such an old story, the eternal triangle and I am the rejected lover, beating her breast, wallowing in pain, how trite, how mundane, it's Crisco on the toothbrush, it's moldy white bread, it's a sink of dirty dishes, it's a rat inside my head.

I remember when I started to unravel, I had let myself into your place with the key you gave me, I wanted to surprise you, I wanted you to find me naked in your bed. It was cold in your apartment. I was reading John Cheever under the covers, then I got up and went to your closet looking for a blanket and found instead, under some towels, a big, black rubber penis covered with Vaseline. I knew right away it was a dildo though I had never seen one before, it blew me away. I remember how I took it out of the closet, it was still warm, and put it on your kitchen table. I took off my engagement ring and stuck it right on the Vaselined tip and drove weeping home on the expressway, it was a wonder I wasn't killed, you called me on the telephone when you came in. You were frantic, you said you loved me, why should I care what you stuck up your ass, you said you brought the dildo because you wanted to control your urges, you didn't want to go with men anymore, we reconciled, we didn't speak of the dildo incident again, but it was never the same for me after that, I began to find fault with you, to look for weakness, now I wouldn't care if you had a hundred dildos in every color of the rainbow, I wouldn't care if you had a dildo tree, if only we could sit together and drink coffee, take long walks, tell each other stories, if only you still had eyes for me.

C. SVOCUEK

Blessings

Blessing Poem

Blessed be the raspberry jam enema,
blessed be the crackhead shamans walking on the moon,
blessed be black vinyl crotchless panties,
blessed be Poetry – the last chance saloon.
Bless the whiskers still growing on the scrotum of dead Walt
Whitman and the noble heart of Herbert Huncke.
Bless Shakespeare who wrote, "when my love says she is true,
I do believe her though I know she lies."
Bless the tattoos that say
Mother, tattoos that say *Motherfucker*
and the eyes that say *No one home.*
Bless the suicides and bless the perpetual erection,
which is suicide.
Bless the premature ejaculator, the compulsive masturbater
and going down the UP escalator because it is the story of my life,
Bless the seamless absolution of frantic solitary orgasm at three a.m.,
and bless keeping the needle in the vein until
the blood turns to holy water.
Bless the ratty garters holding up the loopy edges of impossible desire
and bless hope against all odds a.k.a. God.
Bless the women who want to be men and have the balls to do it,
bless the cynics, the pigs, the old farts, the young farts,
bless farts of all ages.
Bless men that share the cost of condoms and are excited by
    nipple hair,
I have nipple hair.
Bless the ardent ascent of astonishment, getting it up one more time,
bless the crotch smellers and the secret cellars of my psyche where
I commit imaginary murders and take revenge against false friends.
Bless time without end, ego loss and butt holes that smell like
    chocolate.
Bless John Lennon, Bob Marley and Groucho Marx,
bless pigeons, peacocks, whippoorwills, storks and skylarks,
bless the lovers that never left me alone and crying in the dark.
Bless rhinoplasty, septic tanks, Santa Claus and Snow White,
Bless the night.

Crazy Love Blessing

Bless this moody tit in my mouth whether I like it or not,
this burning in me like an endless cigarette,
this ocean of champagne running out between my legs,
bless this love twisting my nipples until they ache and sing out
Holy Mary, Mother of God,
Glory, Glory Hallelujah and Shake, Rattle and Roll,
bless this love tonguing my asshole,
bringing me jellybeans,
farting in my bed.

Bless this opened gas jet in my head,
this heightened awareness that makes every
second taste like heroin and every minute look like
pink and blue cotton candy,
bless this love that keeps spitting in my eye with its
messy need and greasy dishes,
its cunt lapping, cock sucking dominance games and death wishes,
bless my lover's dirty, old gray socks sleeping
under my bed like two pet mice,
bless his double headed dildo and his ex-wife.

Bless my lover's sperm stink,
bless his tongue in my sink,
his analingus concerto,
his libido in my larynx,
his larva in my lotus,
his elbow in my Jell-O,
bless Tristan und Isolde, Desdemona and Othello,
bless my come in his face, bless his come in my face,
bless taking sex off a leash,
bless fucking for world peace.

Tough Love Blessing

Blessed be the ones who came right out and said they wanted it,
blessed be the ones that smelled like Genoa salami, smegma,
dirty socks, Gorgonzola cheese,
bless those who like to bite and slap and tongue and tease,
bless the one who puts his finger in your ass as you are coming
and the one who pricks your nipple and sucks your blood,
bless all the rancid grease that oils the springs of tough love.
Bless the golden showers that washed me clean,
the bottomless jars of Vaseline,
Bless the mercy fuck that gets you through the night,
the fixed fight, the rat in the rectum,
the gynecologists cold metal speculum.
Bless ignoring the rules and stopping the game.
Bless the out and out bastards, the uptight pricks,
but do not bless the hypocrite or prana sucker
who says one thing and means another.
Bless Marquis de Sade's mother, tit clamps, lubricated rubbers,
bless T.S. Eliot who wrote
April is the cruelest month,
full of memory and desire,
bless the sixty year old nymphomaniac and sex-for-hire,
bless the slaves to Diet Pepsi and dominant Duck,
bless vinegar douches and endless sucks,
bless the foolish hope in the word "Neo,"
the erection as hard as stainless steel.
Bless the iron hand in the iron glove,
bless tough love.

Art Blessing

Bless exploding the spectrum,
bless the video camera in God's rectum making great art,
bless art that bounces us against the roof
like an old car with no shocks,
bless art that is hard cock.
Bless the clean brush,
the hush that comes before
the darkness catches flame,
the screaming demons inside you
that drive you to the top of your game
and bless the zipless fuck that
is your fifteen minutes of fame.
Bless art that does not buy or sell,
art that nothing can tame,
art that leaves you blushing, rushing,
seething, feeding, exalted, defenseless.
Bless the destruction of all academic and compulsive agendas,
bless Georgia O'Keefe and her flowering pudendas.
Bless Allen Ginsberg who wrote:
the skin is holy, the nose is holy,
the eyeball is holy, the abyss is holy,
holy are the crazy shepherds of rebellion.
Bless all the artists,
artists who paint Elvis on velvet,
sculptors with no fingers or thumbs,
Bless Francis Bacon and R. Crumb,
Bless art yuppies, acrylic wannabes,
ersatz Van Goghs in Kostabi clothes
who will never be strong enough to cut off an ear,
Bless the life of the struggling artist, the thrift store jeans,
no medical insurance, perpetual rice and beans,
and all that keeps you going is the way
each idea leads to the next idea.
Bless cyber art, outsider art, graffiti art, lost art,
minimalist art, maxed-out art, dumb art, smart art,
the goldmine, moonshine power of art that makes you feel.
Bless the art of fantasy, the art of the real.

Vagina Blessing

Bless the concept of the eternal mother,
her teats like twin mountains,
her mammoth, cavernous udders,
her regal blue-violet vagina
opening into the night tent of the sky,
bless the power of the cosmic cervix,
the healing douche that lives within
its blind forgiving eye.
Bless the connoisseurs of vagina,
the Casanovas, the rookies, the soft donuts,
the tough cookies,
bless the cranberry courtesy of the clitoris,
its crooning valentine.
Bless the magic carpet I see when I look
between my legs,
bless the eternal mystery of the eggs.
Bless all the words for vagina that are supposed
to be dirty but are not:
cunt, clit, pussy, hole, snatch, twat.
Bless the holy sluts and bless the knowledge that
all sluts are holy,
bless cunt smells: fish, cabbage soup,
blood, pumpernickel, caramel.
Bless the autonomy of the vagina:
its ability to choose,
its good taste in umbrellas,
its better taste is shoes.
Bless the variety of the vagina,
its size, colors, uses: file cabinet, winning bet, castenet,
snake charmer, shock absorber, foot warmer.
Bless a short fuse in my manifold of desire,
motor oil in my clit, vulva fire,
bless taking it harder and harder,
longer and longer
and bless taking it higher.

Blessing for the New Year

Blessed be the undescended testicle, the lumpy ungainly breast,
the bunion, the distended uterus,
bless false teeth, dry pussy, limp cocks,
bless the prison of the unloved body and
the magic leap of faith that opens the locks.
Bless the vast colonies of forlorn desire and
all the pilgrims who died there.
Bless everyone blinded by beauty and everyone
who farted in the middle of the school prayer.
Bless cunt hair, penis pie, and the self-righteous freaks
who think they understand the universe because they get high.
Bless the suspenders of judgement, the extenders of clemency,
the Maidenform 42 DD, the hermaphrodite Gods of Androgyny
and spitting in the face of hypocrisy.
Bless the bastard in bastardy, the hysteric in hysterectomy,
the leper in leprosy
and the transcendence in LSD.
Bless all the toilets and shit buckets in the world.
Bless the pursuit of the perpetual orgasm when it is
not a get rich scheme,
bless K-Y jelly and Koromex cream.
Bless the invisible synapses of hope that connect us to
the experiential world, bless peep shows and shy little girls,
bless the old rooster who has nothing left but crow,
the young cock who doesn't know he doesn't know
and the crack in the glass that leads to worlds unknown.
Bless the egg rolling off the table particularly when I am that egg,
Bless the bottom of the glass and all the dregs,
bless bees-wax, borax and the milky way,
Bless New Years Day.

Short List Blessing Poem

Bless my flushing toilet,
bless my African violets,
bless the silk gauntlet of flesh,
the breast, the neck of fellow feeling
that is the tissue of love.
Bless all the books on my shelf
and all the tricks of self deception I have invented
without which I could not get by.
Bless thrift stores, Nyquil, wine coolers and
all cheap highs.
Bless Joel Litzky, Bruce Karan, Steven Laslo.
Bless holding on to this dear life
and bless letting go.

Kamikaze Lover

My ex-lover says you brought this on yourself,
my dope dealer says smoke chiba-chiba for mental health
but I'm so far gone I'm still trying to love myself.
I'm the kamikaze poet,
lost in Xanadu with Coleridge,
drowning with Hart Crane,
dancing with Jack Micheline,
selling poems in the rain.

I am the mumbo-jumbo Walt Whitman in the gumbo poet,
the teapot in the icebox, gravel in my girdle poet,
the living proof a witch loses her powers
when she falls in love poet.
I am the finger in your ass poet
who lives inside everyone, the kamikaze lover poet,
eulogizer of kamikaze love.
I write my poems with my wet dreams,
my screw ups, my come.
Pomposity for a year and holy for a day,
I'm Phi Beta Kappa, school of interrupted foreplay.
I want to explode my loneliness into a fire on the page,
I'm inspired by rage, motivated by serial rejections.
I am the poet of vanished erections,
the web-footed wordsucker,
the bardic duck in your pond of despair.
I'll draft goofy love songs
from the knots in your pubic hair.
My kamikaze love is better than guzzling Krispy Kreme Donuts
in an empty room,
kiss me and I'll commit hari-kari in your Fruit of the Looms.

Campaign Speech

I'm running for President of the next millennium.
My platform is satin sheets on every bed,
stop chasing street artists, go after Disney instead.
I advocate kicking over all the traces,
cross-pollination of the races,
banning bombs, sharing bread.
I'm the AC-DC, l-m-n-o-p candidate, lone-wolf candidate,
werewolf candidate,
I'm gonna howl my way into your head.
I celebrate accordion vagina as well as tight cunt,
I celebrate truth, motherhood and keeping the Mojo up front.
My greatest hope is a global website with the password Trust,
I want to replace the mercy fuck with respect
for the luck of the draw,
and the quick fix with a sustaining dream of true love.
Everyone will get a second and third chance –
there will be no ceiling on born again romance.
I've trained for the job by being a beggar,
a go-between, a go-fer, a fool, a fop, a not-so-Zen whore.
My libido has been overmasturbated,
I'm flat chested, constipated, the perfect candidate,
a twice-divorced ex-psychedelic punk with
Astroglide in my medicine pouch,
if elected I will send the thought police south,
put the food of human kindness in every mouth.
I will release all political prisoners and make everyone
a member of Congress.
I will outlaw all yellow bellied hypocrites,
all one-way streets, all quota systems,
all West Point cadets, all buy-now, pay-later plans,
all interrupted orgasms, all pay toilets and light beer.

I can not promise a self-cleaning carburetor, a heavenly elevator,
an ice cream truck, but you will get a rubber duck,
a Bronx cheer, a poker chip,
a cupcake in your panties
and a world without censorship.

Dead Colette's Song

How I miss Cheri with his long, hard thighs, his willow waist,
his ardent spine that played beneath my fingers like a piccolo.
He was a strong, shining blade,
I danced beneath him like Sheherazade,
teasing him with veils of perfume, first the perfume of violets,
purple as the marks my mouth put on his neck,
then the burning perfume of my tears,
salty, sharp as my fear that time,
that bitch coquette with her iron corset,
would take him before I could taste him.
I covered him with forget-me-nots,
the petals of orchids and the sweet mocha paste
at the bottom of a cup of chocolate.
I curled my tongue along his leg,
licked the spice from his jolie fleur,
bit down until he cried,
I held him till he bled,
marked him, branded him mine.

Je suis Colette, I have no regrets.
I miss the pretty Egyptian boys I used to buy for thirty sous
and the maroon velvet sofas swollen with gossip and intrigue,
I miss them too.
I miss my little dog Fifi and the soft pink breasts of Gigi
and Soutine, Claudine, Mitsou and Mimi, the tart
with the voice of a lark.
I miss *les mushrooms sauté* and *les oysters grille*
and how Missy and I played tag in the park.
We smoked cigarillos, wore tuxedos,
she was my tiger lily, I was her pussy willow.

Je suis Colette, je n'ai rien de regret,
Mes livres etaient lu par tout le monde.
I danced the tarantula before the king of Sweden,
bared my breast so he could kiss it.
I never wasted a rendezvous
or spilled champagne on a friend.

I took my fourteen year old stepson into his father's den
and for starters, showed the boy how to undo my garters.
I left no fruit untasted,
sucked the wells of love and laughter dry
and one day lined my eyes,
set out my pens, and then, I died.

Valentine

I love romantic euphemisms for big cocks
like passion pistols and monster rocks.
I love all the long hairs and short hairs of hot romance,
so I dress up my little monkey in pink lace underpants.
I love combing your pelt with my tongue, snickering like a baboon,
until I get you howling at the moon.
I love other people's children, other people's cats,
other people's false assumptions that
I regret one second of my chaotic erotic past.
I love the relentless honesty of mirrors,
the anarchic marginality I choose to live in,
and being wholly committed to getting what I need for myself.
I bathe in sweet cream and drink top shelf.
I love celebrating the aphrodisiac powers of gin,
I love knowing faking an orgasm is the only carnal sin.
My disappointments in bed have taught me
mind and body are one and if there is such a thing as true love:
it's making your partner come – any way you can:
phone sex, three fingers, a thumb.
I love capitulation as much as I love the joy of the hunt.
I love knowing all philosophies are meaningless
except the harmony of cock and cunt.
As much as I love the teachings of the Buddha,
I love the straight forward contract of sex-for-hire,
I am willing to relinquish all desire except the desire for desire.
I love to join the hungry bodies cruising
in the late night bus stations of unbridled lust.
I love the abolition of all obligatory words like *ought to,*
have to, should and *must.*
I love eating the cherries out and leaving the crust.

Ass Wish List

I want a pink leather evening dress with a slit in back
cut so high up you can see the dimples in my sacroiliac.
I want an ass that never stops bouncing,
I want a bad ass,
I want an ass juicier than a room full of ripe watermelons,
I want an ass that can fuck the "in" out of indifference,
an ass that can sing acappella,
I want an ass that sings so loud it drowns out the sound
of constipated hypocrites,
I want to wrap my ass around the New York Knicks,
I want a pair of giant opera glasses
made of all seeing microchips so
I can see all the freckles on the backside of the moon,
I want to only eat the asses of honest men,
I want to rim the cosmic asshole with my tongue,
I want to have the courage to keep my ass wide open
for whatever comes,
I want to have a pet-turtle named "Hard-Ass"
(and another one named "Hard-On").
I want to die in the middle of writing a poem.
I want to bring everyone's ass home.

Shining Sapphire Star Buddha of Satori Sex Prayer

Sacred shekinah splendid Sinbad Shangri-la,
shooting, shining, sapphire star Buddha of Satori Sex,
teach me to cut my losses, hedge my bets,
teach me not to mistake conversation for foreplay.
Ass kissing Buddha with your plastic smiles,
release me from the twisted maze of my own innuendoes.
Teach me to say just what I mean,
Piss in the Beer Buddha of Split Infinitives
Cum in Your Face Dreams.

Low Self-Esteem Buddha on your shaky throne,
with your tentative similies and halting poems,
teach me not to reject other souls
when their desperation reminds me of my own.
Buddha of Crossing the Line,
barbaric stiletto Buddha of the Serpentine,
triple dicked Buddha of Saber-Tooth Sex
with your Mick Jagger mouth and fourteen breasts,
Rubber Room Strap-On Buddha,
Buddha of Black Latex,
teach me to suspend judgement,
teach me acceptance,
stoke my jets.

Meditation on Dirty Laundry

I love dirty laundry, I love how it smells,
I love funky, toe-cheesy socks that remind me
of happy feet running around town,
I love dirty mens tee-shirts, that rank underarm smell,
it's so sexy, that smell of honest sweat,
when it's combined with grease or motor oil,
there's nothing like it,
so, if you know any mechanics or bikers,
please ask them to give you a dirty tee-shirt for me,
the best would be one they wore three or four days,
and then there's panties, my own panties,
just smelling my own panties when I take them off
after a busy day brings me to the point of orgasm.
I don't do the laundry very often,
I like to let the laundry pile up in my big laundry bag
and if I come home tired and blue, the first thing
I do is head for the laundry bag, open it up,
take a great, big sniff, it revives me,
the scent and stink of life gets me high as a kite,
I love that dirty laundry.

SIN

One cigarette,
half of a sugar cookie
(the part with the chocolate icing),
me chasing after you, wetting my pants,
my heart in my hand.

Ode to Balls

Balls, balls, balls, I love them all,
big hairy sacs and cute little peanut balls,
veiny, grainy, hangdog balls, puffy, scruffy balls,
even sweaty, stinky, sticky toe-cheesy balls,
balls, I love them all.
Balls shaped like boxing gloves,
balls hanging from the clouds above,
balls skipping rope,
balls eternal hope,
furry, fantastic, beautiful, elastic,
bombastic, spastic balls,
balls, balls – I love them all.

Neo-Feminine Resistance Rant

I resist wearing white cotton panties,
I will only wear pink silk, see-through black nylon,
red lace,
I resist saying I'm straight
when like Curt Cobain,
I believe everyone is gay,
I resist the brittle limitations of any one category;
I want to be your bitch, your whore,
your baby, your mama, your daddy, your best friend,
your doctor, your nurse, your enema, your sponge bath,
your sofa cushion, your janitor,
your landlady and your back door.
I resist collusion, compromise and complicity
as I resist the role of mediator, appeaser
or cockteaser,
I resist latté
I resist plastic wrapping my emotions
and hiding my anger
like a half eaten sandwich
in the back of the refrigerator,
I resist abandoning the ideals
of sisterhood and brotherhood,
Robin Hood and Johnny Be-Goode.
as I resist poodles and pom-poms,
vinegar douches, frou-frous and peeping Toms.
I resist seeing menstruation as oppression
no matter how bad the cramps,
I resist breast implants and sunlamps
as I resist weeping or cringing or wringing my hands
or clinging to anything but the truth
that we need each other.
I resist being anything but butch in my backbone
while I always try my best to dress like a heart breaking femme,
and when I come, when I come,
I always want to come
like a woman in love.
I resist power trips and Mr. Clean,
skinny hips, gossip and size queens.

C. SKOCZEK

Good Bye Beautiful Mother

Dying Mother Poem

At the nursing home I lift my old mother,
her bones rustle inside her skin like seeds in a pod.
I move her from the wheelchair to the bed,
swing her legs up, straighten her head,
the whites of her eyes are yellow as if glazed with urine,
her ragged breath scratches me like a whisper.
Ma, I say, I have good news, my book is going to be published.
She says, suddenly, in her old, firm voice,
that's wonderful, I'm happy for you.
Then her head lolls back, spittle on her lips.
Ma, ma, I say, but she is not there.

On her good days,
they prop her up in her wheelchair with pillows
(she does not remember how to sit).
They wheel her to a corner of the dining room, near a window.
All day long she sits there, yelling, let's go, let's go, hurry, hurry.
They say they must segregate her
because her constant noise disturbs the others.
I think they are afraid she will start an insurrection
and the others will take up her cry — let's go, hurry.

My mother once chased me all over the house,
hitting me with her broom,
yelling, witch, witch!
That was when she found the diaphragm in my sock drawer.

When the nurse changed my mother, she said,
Please missy, turn over,
but this was just a courtesy
because my mother cannot move.
There is something so ugly and selfish in my grief.
I don't ever want to be like her the way she is now
and I didn't want to be like her when she was younger,
sweeping constantly, cleaning the house,
staying up all night in the basement,
sewing clothes for other women

for money to buy me a leather jacket
or send my brother to camp.
I want her to punish me for the contempt I had for her,
to yell and hit me with her broom
but it's too late, too late now.

Watching Television

My mother is dying and all I can do is watch television
as I wait for a call from Maryland telling me to come down
and sit by her hospital bed.
I watch *As the World Turns* until my brother calls,
says it's a false alarm, a urinary tract infection.
They will treat her and send her back to the nursing home,
she will be kept alive by force feeding as she has forgotten how to
    swallow.
I can not swallow keeping her alive like this,
her throat a tube they push food through,
her fine breasts shrunk to pits, her legs useless sticks.
I tell my father that force feeding her is sadistic and cruel.
He says I can't just let mom die.
He gives the nursing home permission, although her living will says
she did not want her life prolonged by artificial means.
The director of the nursing home says despite the living will
my father is the guardian.
My brother says lay off the old man, you're driving him crazy,
but the last time I visited I held my mother's cold hand as she slept,
every few minutes she screamed in her sleep ow, ow, ow...

Suddenly she opened her eyes, raised her head, looked right at me:
I need your help badly, she said.
Then her eyes shut, her head rolled back,
my wise mother who always knew best
although I consistently ignored what she had to say,
had to find out for myself there is the devil to pay,
when I get off the phone with my brother,
I go back and sit in front of the television as easily
as a bird returns to its nest.
Since my mother got sick I watch a lot of television.
It fills up the black hungry holes in my head.
All this would make a good script for soap opera,
at the part where my mother says I need your help,
the background music swells to Scheherazade,
I roll out my magic carpet, gather my mother up
and we soar through the roof into a fine, blue sky.

While magic realism is making some headway on TV,
there are no buyers for this script, so everyday
I get on the phone and beg my father to let my mother die.

During the commercial, they sell new cars, soda, armchairs.
I unzip my jeans, invade my underpants,
put my fingers inside my crotch,
my mother used to call it a lily,
but no matter what I call it,
I find no comfort there.
Like my mother's hand,
it is cool, thin, dry.

Beautiful Craziness

When I wouldn't play with the dolls he bought me, and instead
drew crayon pictures of horses with breasts and wings,
my father said he was afraid I'd grow up crazy
and end up in Kings County psych ward like his artistic sister Mae.
When I told my father it was barbaric to put my mother on a
    feeding tube,
he said I was crazy, it would be barbaric *not* to, but
at the last minute he decides against the feeding tube,
tells the hospital no.
My mother will be sent back to the nursing home,
taken off medication,
she will be given morphine,
proving there is still mercy in the world.

Maybe he realized I was right or maybe my brother told him I said
if they put the tube in, kept my mother alive like
she was a goose being fattened for paté, I'd go down there,
smother her with a pillow,
and my father thinks I'm crazy enough to do it.
My father doesn't know that imagination is real;
he doesn't believe in karma
or the magnificence of the universe.
He wants to spend his old age watching sports on TV
but that does not mean he is not right about me,
I am crazy.
How beautiful this crazy is, it turns me into a fly on the wall,
I can go anywhere,
I can hear my ex lying about me a thousand miles away,
I can see the blood running in my veins
darker than wine – same type as my mother's – rare type O,
I can say anything,
I can say I give the best head in North America,
I can lie about my age, my name,
even threaten to kill my mother
when I haven't the courage to kill a cockroach.
As any visitor to my apartment will tell you,
I make jokes about collecting them.

My mother collected things; little porcelain teacups, brass camels
from Morocco, matchbooks from weddings, bar mitzvahs, motels.
Once I asked her why, she said she didn't know,
maybe she was trying to keep a diary of her life.
I do not have the patience for collecting.
Instead I write, piecing words
together like a crazy quilt
as if that could hide me from the night.

Angel Wings

My mother's hands are spread out
before her on the thin, blue hospice blanket
like angel wings in the sky.
Soon, I think,
I will be hearing heavenly choirs.

I am very glad there is a joint
in my backpack
which I will smoke
in the bathroom of the Amtrak
in approximately an hour
on the way home.

My mother's eyes are open
yet she does not seem to see,
she opens her mouth,
makes a sound, calls out a word,
but she has not spoken sense in a month.

I lean my cheek on the rail of the hospital bed,
my mother speaks:
shoetree,
she calls out to the cosmos,
and then *telephone*
and a few minutes later, *Mildred*,
the name of her dead sister,
Mildred, and then *light, star, comb*.
My father comes into the room buttoning his jacket
"I don't want to hit rush hour on the Beltway,"
he says, "let's go."
"I love you ma," I say
and kiss her on her waxy mouth.
She says—*I know*.

On the Day Before My Mother Died

In the morning
on a street
so high up in Manhattan,
so foreign
it could be Canada,
I see a black cat
seated directly ahead,
crossing my path,
I get close and find out
it is not a cat at all,
but a swollen, plastic garbage bag
that could hold anything,
even a pile of bones.

These Changes Are Physiological

Because the train was held over
half an hour in Philadelphia
I get to the hospice
ten minutes after my mother dies.

I can not bring myself to kiss her mouth,
it is open, gaping,
dark as a charnel pit,
so I kiss her cheek and find it
still warm.

My father and brother leave
to get some sleep
and I wait with her for the undertaker.
I hold her hand,
after a while it cools.
Her color changes, pales, fades.
She caves in
like a balloon that has been punctured.

If there is such a thing as a soul,
it has left her body
but I know these changes are physiological
because I read it in a book.

When the undertaker comes
I don't want him to take her,
I want to hold her hand forever
but I help him lift her up
into the black bag on top of the gurney,
it is then I see that her small pink feet
have changed
into the long, yellow toes
of a jackal.

Rose Medallion

My mother collected rose medallion china; stately court scenes:
a king listening to musicians, ladies in elegant robes drinking tea,
painted in varied shades of rose and green, each plate a dream
     about a lost world.
She kept adding to her collection through heartbreak and betrayal.
When her favorite sister cracked up, she brought a sugar bowl,
when I aborted her grandchild she acquired a platter showing
royal children flying kites.

After she and my father moved to Maryland,
she worked doing alterations for a famous department store.
She added better pieces to her collection; fluted vases, teapots,
     soup tureens.
She bought a mahogany china closet carved with dragons
for her treasures.
She was the rose medallion queen.
Her beautiful collection reflected the serenity she displayed
in this period of her life, before her terrible sickness.
When I visited in those golden days,
she would offer me any piece in her collection,
I want to give you something special, she said.
I persistently refused her generous offer, finally,
opted for something else,
a venetian glass bowl that had belonged to her mother.
I could never accept what she wanted to give me,
would only take her love on my terms,
establishing a pattern for accepting affection
that has scarred my life with loneliness.

Now when I go see my father in what was their home
I sit with him on the couch,
pretending to listen as he talks about his health,
all the while my eyes are fixed on her fabulous cabinet,
her collection crowded on the shelves.
The ornate china looks fussy, overdone, baroque,
and I wonder if she loved rose medallion because
it is exquisitely composed, everything is in it's proper place,
an effort to order chaos, a triumph of grace.

A Jewel Wrapped in Plastic

It fell to me to go through her things,
she had left little notes, i.e. inside the front cover;
please save this book,
it has beautiful artwork in it.

Her handwriting was as always,
cramped, precise, left to right,
nothing to indicate she would soon
forget how to make a cup of tea.
I can never know when
she started making the notes:
when she first felt her memory go
or when she got the diagnosis: Alzheimers.
Oh no, she cried out in the Doctors office,
this means I'm going to lose my mind.

She always held the pen very tight,
the way she held her feelings inside,
I saw her cry once;
at the funeral of her favorite brother,
then she brushed the tears away with the back of her wrist,
pulled her lips shut tight as a zipper.

Her good jewelry was in a plastic bag in a purse in her closet,
each piece carefully tucked into a smaller plastic bag,
each with it's little note,
for granddaughter Julia a perfect string of pearls,
a silver butterfly for me,
a topaz heart set in gold with a note:
yellow is your color.

Now, I see with two pairs of eyes,
hers and mine, all colors doubly radiant,
and my life ever more precious,
each day a treasure protected by her love,
like a jewel wrapped in plastic
to save it from scratches.

February 2

Groundhog's day,
your birthday today mother,
first winter you are down in the earth,
this morning, the newscaster on the radio
said the groundhog, Punxsutawney Phil,
saw his shadow
there will be six more weeks of winter,

I go to the sauna,
where even sweating
in 212 degree heat,
there is winter inside me,
a dead cold place.
I think of your fine bones crumbling,
turning to dust,
I sweat and shower, sweat and shower
but can not wash away
the feeling of dirt on my face.
.
When I go home I get out my yoga mat,
put on my yoga clothes,
I push myself through the usual poses,
the lion, the cobra, wheel, frog, the crow.
At the end of my workout
I do the shoulderstand and
then I am a candle to you, mother,
my inverted arms make the base,
my legs the candlestick,
I reach up with my toes to make the wick
and imagine I'm a flame
burning your name
in the black sky of time.

Good Bye Beautiful Mother

Good bye hyacinth,
satin skin,
cheekbones wide as Asia
that made you look like Kwan Yin
though you drove yourself
without mercy,
good bye amber eyes,
graceful fingers
always moving,
working, sewing,
stitching through the air
a week before your death
embroidering your funeral dress,
good bye fertile navel that grew me,
soft belly that held me,
yoni that opened to accept my seed,
how you tried to hold me,
control me,
how I struggled to define myself
against what you thought was real,
you were the crucible that made me,
hot as fire,
true as steel,
beautiful mother,

good bye ferocious pride,
good bye vanilla pudding pie,
feet size $5\frac{1}{2}$,
staccato laugh,
good bye humming bird, good bye.

L. SKOCZEK

Why Do Yoga?

Why Do Yoga?

Spine cracks,
bones ache,
getting harder and harder
to do the frog,
the locust,
the plow,
why persist in this,
is it masochism
to push myself so?
Do I actually think
this can somehow slow
the long inevitable slide
into darkness?

I don't know,
but now
breathing deep,
exhausted,
in corpse position
on the floor,
I see reflected
in the mirror
by the door,
a window of sky.

Sunday Morning Yoga

Doing Sunday morning yoga
in my sunny room,
I assume the bound lotus pose,
I think about my husband
who won't sign the divorce papers
though we haven't seen each other in two years.
When we married he always wanted us to watch
porn tapes when we were screwing,
said that's what he and his first wife
used to do.

I move out of bound lotus onto
my hands and knees for cat pose,
I arch my back,
I can get into some porn and hootchie-koo,
but every time?
sometimes I wanted him to look at me,
not a lithe, redhead giving oral pleasure
to a big, black man.
When I tried to talk about it,
we would fight
and run away from each other.
Soon the porn tapes stayed in a burlap sack
in his closet,
now and then, when he wasn't home
I'd get one out and watch it,
I'd soon feel that familiar heat bubbling
between my legs,
then I'd bring myself off
abruptly with a frantic, rough hand.

From cat pose, all I have to do
is bow my back and I'm in cow pose,
supposed to inspire patience
and acceptance of your lot.

If I was on top,
he often put a pillow over his head,
furious, but still excited,
I would continue until I brought us both to orgasm
all the while wondering if he was imagining
a nymphet with watermelon breasts,
in this way our sex life became
a lethal, withholding game.

I move from cow into easy pose,
which is seated, cross legged,
spine relaxed,
this helps to quiet the restless soul.
I drink some water,
continue through my paces,
I do the lion for courage,
the bow pose for centering
the wheel for harmony between
body and soul.
Now he doesn't want to sign
the divorce papers,
he wants to come down from Canada
and talk about it,
I tell him I have nothing left to say.
I rest for five minutes on my yoga mat,
in baby pose,
listen to the easy, natural rhythm
of my breath,
then I place the top of my head on the floor
in preparation for the peacock,
as I kick my legs out behind me
and spread them wide open
like a fan
I wonder if
pornography is the opposite of tantra.

A Better Skin

I do yoga
trying to stretch
into a better skin.
I pull my bones out of my sockets,
I push my navel towards heaven,
if there is such a place,
I open my knees, my thighs,
I want to wash the hollow
between my legs with air.

Before waking in the morning
I find myself dreaming about yoga
in the way one does
about a lost lover,
I see my body rising up
embracing
what it yearns for.

In the conscious world
this meaning eludes me,
but still I try to wed
oceans of spirit and flesh.

I want to glide through my yoga
with effortless grace,
like a soul on ice skates,
but I sweat, groan, curse,
have to stop, drink water,
rest,
I know this is the devil's test,
testing to see if my being is stronger
than my body.

Medusa

I buy a postcard Medusa
at St. Marks bookstore.
Standing under an angry gray sky,
she is wearing red lipstick, smiling,
her hair a mass of wiry black snakes.

This modern Medusa
doesn't look like a monster,
she is too beautiful,
but I have learned how
monsters are good at disguises,
just as I have learned
many men think
women are monsters,
with teeth sprouting from our labia,
our vaginas dentata,
that is why they must make myths
out of us
and have been doing so
since the beginning of time.

I can not be an ivory Aphrodite
worshipped for her genius and beauty
or a happy streetwalker
with a rosebush between my legs,
an updated version of Henry Miller's Germaine,
for better or worse,
my mind and body are the same,
I understand why people
kill for love,
like Medusa, I have cobras on the brain,
but I don't want to turn men to stone with my face
or wield the terrible power of my sex
before me like a shield,

I would rather be Teiresias,
blind, hermaphrodite prophet,
doomed to speak
only what I can hear and feel,

in the exploding fires
of the sexual embrace
not even the gods know
what is real.

Christmas Eve Subway Conversation

Found poem overheard on the A train to Brooklyn

Man 1: Hey Man, how you doing?

Man 2: O.k., yourself?

Man 1: Still working for the transit, how about you?

Man 2: Yeah, but I got a bad problem with that woman. I'm going there now, try to do right by my kids. She's not gonna stop me getting them their Christmas toys. That's what's in this plastic bag.

Man 1: You and she split up?

Man 2: Yeah, she got one of those court orders against me. I got a way of dealing with women. I'll compromise but you gotta listen to me, why you with me if you won't listen to me?

Man 1: But the women now, they won't listen.

Man 2: That's what happen, I was just trying to talk to her. She wouldn't listen, kept yakking at me, had to hit her up against the head a couple of times, just to make her quiet, you know.

Man 1: That was when she got one of those court orders against you?

Man 2: Right, thirty days in Rikers and I had to take a course about domestic violence, she the one should be taken it, all her yaking made me violent, cost me plenty, now see these bags, they filled with toys for my boys. The biggest one he be nine years and then I got another one with her, five years old. I'm gonna call her from the street, ask her to come down and meet me, and if she don't I'll find me a cop and he'll come up with me and deliver 'em. I'll do it if I have to, that woman she turned bad on me. She got a girlfriend you know, single one, she always over the house, talking bad about me.

Man 2: Ah, now I got the picture.

Man 1: Man never knows what's gonna happen when those women get talkin'.

Man 2: Ain't that the truth….

On Not Going to Gregory Corso's Funeral

"You should go to the funeral," Steve said last night at dinner.
"Yes," Yuko added, "he was the last of the Beats except for
    Orlovsky."
"But Orlovsky was more Ginsberg's muse than a poet," Donald said,
just then our Pad Thai and shrimp fried rice came,
we dug in and didn't say any more about it,
until we were waiting for the check,
when Steve looked at me and said,
"Yeah, you should go, Patti Smith will be there, she's going to speak."
"Do you think she can help me get an agent?" I asked him.
"Very funny," Steve said,
"O.k., what time?" I asked.
"9:30 a.m." he told me.

The one time I saw Gregory Corso, he was at a crowded reading
    at St. Marks,
wearing a big, heavy, dark brown overcoat though it was spring.
He was medium towards small sized and not physically
    outstanding,
clean shaven with a big mop of graying hair,
standing at the back of the room very drunk and bellowing loudly,
I couldn't make out what about.
The poet on the podium, John Giorno, said "Gregory, pipe down."
that's how I knew it was Gregory Corso.
People around him were trying to calm him, "Shush, shush,"
said his friends, pulling at his arms.
"Come on, Gregory," an intense young man with big wire
    eyeglasses said,
but Gregory was not to be silenced,
he bellowed on, behaving like a poet,
drunken and mad,
like Dylan Thomas, like Baudelaire,
I thought he was wonderful.

I didn't go to Gregory's funeral, even though he wrote,
I knew God would turn back his head
If I sat quietly and thought.
I stayed home, nursed a hangover, drank ginger ale
and thought how my last lover broke it off because he wanted
    someone younger,
how the big literary agent said my manuscript was too confessional,
how my friends were sitting in the pews at the church listening to
    Patti Smith
talk about Gregory Corso.

I thought about what my life would be like if
I could not write poetry, if I could not transform
my sorrows into these little strings of words
to tie around myself to keep from
falling into pieces,
then I thought about the Beats,
how they were comrads and compañeros,
how they wrote about self consciousness
and consciousness of self,
and I thought about Gregory's self,
still at last, like a leaf frozen in snow,
and his big, old overcoat,
Where is it? Who has it now?

Spontaneous Song for Hersch Silverman

Bee-bop, doo-wop, truth breathing, trumpet jamming poet,
fire speaking, high flying, turquoise night dragon poet,
fish swimming upstream in the raging rivers of fear poet,
rollercoaster, carousel, wonder wheel, chamber of mirrors,
    funhouse poet,
ham and cheese on rye as well as alfalfa sprouts
on whole wheat with tomato poet,
with the innocence of a two year-old and
the compassion of ten thousand Buddhas,
poet spitting in the eye of all tyrannies and repression,
poet of mercury, molyblendium, neon, neptunium, titanium,
tungsten, uranium, elemental poet of transmutation,
turning loss-dross to transcendence,
caroling with Blake, Whitman and Ginsberg,
Hersch, reading out your symphonies of words
in coffeehouses to two people,
in smokey bars where no one is listening,
reading in dreams,
Hersch, with your peacock quill soul pen,
writing on the cosmic sky songs of rainbows
and orange, pink, rose, red, ruby sunrise,
tree of life poet,
poet,
Hersch.

Flower Bed

rooting through the compost heap
of dreams and desire,
digging with my fingers and tongue,
I find you ready to penetrate me
like a pick into earth,
breaking new ground,

this awesome act of courage is terrifying,
planting seeds of joy or heartbreak,

we never know what we will find
when we search
inside each other's skin;
the way out or the way in
to the garden of lost souls.

Five Erotic Haiku

May or *Trapped Ball Sack*

Locking my legs around your waist,
I catch the bull frog
in my craw.

My July

Venus retrograde,
pussy flagrante,
glass empty.

September Senryu

I floss my teeth with your ass hair
but you still want me
to tell you
I love you.

November

Thanksgiving in the shower,
your cock scrubs the cranberries
out of my ass.

December

The gifts of the Magi,
your three fingers
stuck up inside me.

Hawkeyed Merlin

I dreamed you were Hawkeyed Merlin arrived to watch over me,
I dreamed you were Lancelot, Robin Hood and Billy the Kid,
I dreamed you were Kurosawa and Dylan Thomas,
I dreamed you were Neal Cassady
picking me up in a sky blue Chevrolet,
I dreamed you were the man who shaved his crotch for me,
I dreamed you were brown hair and Jesus,
I dreamed you were jam,
I dreamed you were the great horned toad, Shiva,
and I was your consort Kali with my ten thousand,
opening thighs,
I dreamed you were the gate out of these fields of loneliness,
I dreamed you were the key to the palace of requited desires,
I dreamed you were Puerto Rico, Madagascar and Sicily,
I dreamed I was your baby, your come-at-last happiness
and you were my joy and holy fire.

Sparkling Water Dream

I dreamed I took my brain out
and washed it in sparkling water,
then I dreamed I was the maiden in the wood
and you were the sacred unicorn,
I dreamed I was the cosmic salad,
you were the oil
I licked off my crisp green fingers,
I dreamed I lived in a democracy
founded on mutuality of pleasure and 69,
I dreamed cock size was not important
and no one was afraid to use lube.
I dreamed everyone was allowed to keep their
little plate of happiness.

I dreamed the setting sun behind the Statue of Liberty
made scarlet mandalas of kissing mouths,
and the body was holy ground
each act of coitus a shared and sacred pilgrimage,
I dreamed yoni gardens and fields where
lingams grew high as cherry trees,
I dreamed I was the honeysuckle
and you were the bumble bee.

God Rant

I don't want a credit card God, a greedy dickhead God
with a gold money clip between his legs,
I don't need his shiny, plastic love
to buy me bully dicks, leather whips, silicon tits,
or a gigolo in a hotel room.
I don't need Jehovah, Lord God King of the Universe,
that massive ego trip designed
to crush me into a Jell-O pancake,
and forget the martyred saints:
Joan of Arc burned at the stake,
or Jesus, the presumptive baby son of God
with his shabby mythologies
of resurrection and eternal life.
I reject the God of Allah, his flaming knives,
bloody hands, cemeteries of twisting, shifting sands.
I don't want a God designed to soothe my fear of death,
a Prozac God, a god of crystal meth,
a chemical, con job God to make me feel holy
as long as my stash holds out.
I won't worship Kali with her centipede legs,
or the earth goddess or the cosmic egg,
I don't even want the compassionate Buddha so
popular with some of my friends.
I don't hope to be seduced by a higher power,
or yearn for Godly absolution in my final hour,
I want to take full responsibility for
my own failures, my futility,
the relentless hostility that makes me torment myself,
my family, my lovers, my friends.
I don't want so called divine redemptive love,
I want world without end,
I want the existential dance:
to walk for centuries with a load in my pants,
to be Obi Wan Kanobe floating up through
infinite galaxies of internal and external space,
to fly up to the milky way on
clouds of human suffering and grace,
maybe I want a perpetual pie in my face,
but I don't want a God.

Witness

"For transgressions against God, the day of atonement atones, for transgressions of one human being against another the day of atonement does not atone until they have made peace with one another." — Midrash

In Union Square after the tragedy,
thousands of people are trying to dispel the darkness,
lighting candles, clasping hands,
singing *Give Peace a Chance*
while the devil does the tarantella through the heavens
holding the earth in his hand like a giant orange.
At any second he may pop it into his mouth
and grind all our unfinished lives into bloody pulp.

Although I believe the words of the Hindu sage Marahanda,
to kill one is to kill ten thousand,
my gut is screaming an eye for an eye, a tooth for a tooth,
get Osama and his hellions, decimate the Mujadhin.
When I tell my Catholic friend Mary, this
she says I feel this way because I am Jewish,
part of an ancient, primitive tribe.
She says it is more evolved to turn the other cheek,
there is nothing more evolved than world peace.
I get furious at her and yell, "When have the Catholics
ever given the world peace?
What about, the inquisition?
What about the popes who believe
that women don't have the right to control their bodies?
The Jews, "I go on, "have given us Freud, Marx, Einstein."
She laughs, "Yes, Einstein," she says, "the father of the atomic bomb."
What about Ghandi? Don't you know that Ghandi was really
    Jewish?" I scream.
She tells me I am insane and she is right.
I AM insane.
Whether my eyes are shut tight or open wide I see,
running over and over in my head, the news clip of the people
jumping out of the windows of the WTC,
their bodies falling like ticker-tape.

I go down to Maryland to spend Yom Kippur with my father.
I sit in the auditorium of the JFK High School
among a thousand, well scrubbed, earnest Jews
dressed in their holiday best.
These Jews are not from my ancient tribe,
they believe in the rule of law – the Torah, the book of laws.
With the rabbi, they bow their heads in a silent prayer for peace.
I hold my head high, savage in my nose ring
and designer knock-offs from H&M
and think that all I believe in is sex and death.
Yet during Kol Nidre, the whisper of wings,
I find myself reaching for my father's hand.

Back in New York, I prepare for the second session
of the erotic writing course I teach.
For the first time in years the course is filled up, eighteen students.
During last weeks introductions, half of them said they took the
course because they wanted to lift their spirits.

I advised them to go out and have some sex.
It would both lift their spirits
and give them something to write about,
I stop my preparations for Class Two: *The Petunia and the Pussy –
    Erotic Language.*
I decide I have to practice what I preach.
I call up a man I have just started to date
but have not yet slept with.
He is as battered as I am but also, astonishingly,
unbroken.
I tell him I have to come over right away.
When I get over there, I stand in front of him
as he sits down on the couch
and I slowly take off my clothes,
he seems startled and lights a cigarette,
but then he gets into it.
He puts the cigarette down into an ashtray and unzips his fly.
He takes his cock out. I like it.
It is solid, thick with desire, upstanding, a tree of life.
He reaches his fingers up and pulls me
down onto him by my nipples.

He has a dog named Abraham Lincoln
he has locked in his darkroom
because I am allergic,
still at the moment of penetration
I feel that itching sensation all over my face
that means I am breaking out in hives,
but I don't let this interrupt our ride.
I concentrate on the heat between us,
the building, cleansing fire.
The Midrash says to search for the sudden light
that lights up the heart.
I do not know about the future of the earth,
I do not know if this sorrow can ever be healed
but at least for this little while I have found what I was hoping for,
there is still miracle and wonder, this is the day of awe.

Baby On The Water

Like Baby Moses, I want to float in a bulrush basket on the river,
I want to be a baby on the water,
smell the sweet, damp swamp earth like
milk on my tongue.
I don't want to know anything about Osama Bin Laden,
anthrax, smallpox, dirty bombs, shoe bombers
or terror alerts on the Brooklyn Bridge,
when I hear the sound of the wind in the tall reeds,
and the pharaoh's daughter approaches with her ladies,
even though I won't understand a word she speaks,
when I hear her voice like silver bells,
I will know I am saved.
I want to be saved by a beautiful princess,
I don't care if she is Egyptian and I am Jewish,
or if her skin is black as the bottom of the Nile
and mine is pale as the tablet on which is written
the Ten Commandments.
All I care about is that she is a beautiful princess who knows
nothing about Jihad or the seven days war or the Gaza Strip,
or suicide bombers at a wedding feast
or the destruction of Palestinian towns.
I dream of being a baby on the water,
of being saved by a beautiful princess,
and when I am grown,
I will move through the centuries.
I won't study the early martyrs,
the Christians who believed the truth will set you free,
when sometimes all the truth will get you is
stabbed in a cathedral like Thomas à Becket,
and I won't study the rabbis
who held the Book of Laws in their arms
while Torquemada burned them at the stake.
I will go out into the desert,
but unlike Moses I won't go up on the mountain,
I don't want to be a giver of laws,
futile laws, empty laws,
laws that tell us there is only one God and he is just,

but do not tell us he is no protection
against nineteen savages with box cutters.
I will wander in the desert,
dragging my rage behind me like a heavy spear,
walking for forty days and forty nights,
forty years, with the hot sands burning my feet,
I will walk and walk until I can smell hope again,
smell hope around me like sweet, damp earth,
walk around till my soul
is no longer weighed down by sorrow and anger,
walk until my soul floats,
floats like a baby on the water.

I Love New York

I love New York, it's a
great, big, beautiful blowjob to the mind
and that's why everyone wants to come here (pun intended).
I love New York it's true America like Wyoming
is true west, only more so.
I love New York with its beautiful symmetry
of Manhattan street grids, the neat criss-cross of east and west
like threads in a fishnet stocking,
and because of four teen boys with a boom box
working the plaza at B'way and 51st ,
and because of the bones of Dee Dee and Joey Ramone,
singing from the stage at CBGB's.
I love New York because of Toys in Babeland
where I can choose between at least 102 different kinds of dildos.
I love New York because I can buy kasha knishes from Mrs. Stahls
out in Brighton Beach or shop for books at the Strand
or go to art shows in Soho where there is a photo
of a young Allen Ginsberg standing naked and grinning
besides an equally naked and grinning Gregory Corso.
I love New York where the streets are paved with spit and sex,
what comes next and fat-tongued voracious hungers,
I love New York because of the tomato plants
growing in a vacant lot on Saratoga Avenue in Brownsville, B'klyn,
I love New York because New York girls have the best legs in the
world, and because of its feuding politicians,
carnival of lying, lice bitten saints,
quick change artists, fan dancers, fly-by-night-jewelers,
drug dealers, gender benders and has been wannabes of all ages,
I love New York, a rhinoceros in the eye of convention,
it's fat as a fart and it screeches like a cat in heat,
it can fool me into thinking
I'll live forever despite the tombstones I see,
growing like forests of Chicklets,
when I am driving north through Queens on the BQE,
I love New York, it's an anarchist nation,
a bump and grind of funky out-of step elation,

I love how the New York night beguiles me,
its dark fingers filled with memories,
I used to see the tarantulas mate with the centipedes
on the old, banished Forty-Second Street.
I love New York, the home of Hiphop and Ralph Kramden,
it bites me, entices me, it's Shanghai on the subway
I get to sit next to sexy, exotic men,
I love New York because before 9/11 I took it for granted
but now I know New York is a hero for our time.
I love New York, it is whiskey in my bottle,
it moves me full throttle, like true love,
like an everlasting, twisting, bitching,
yearning, burning hand in my glove.

Memorial Day

It's Memorial Day, I want to honor our dead soldiers
by writing a happy poem,
I am going to write about orange Popsicles,
about the crisp sugary orange ice,
the taste of that sweet vanilla cream
melting on my tongue,
I don't want to write about threats of terrorist attacks,
saran gas or anthrax,
but about clowns with big, funny, false, red noses
doing cartwheels and somersaults,
tooting their silly honk, honk, honking horns.
I won't mention the clown
running our country who is not smart enough
to graduate from the worst clown school in Siberia.
It's Memorial Day and I'm going to write about
backyard barbecues, hot dogs,
corn on the cob,
and though it's a little early,
I hear this year's corn is particularly sweet,
though perhaps not in the same way
that life seems particularly sweet
when you have managed to slam the brakes on
just before hitting the car in front of you
that has stopped short for no apparent reason.
I will write about how much fun it is
on a summer evening like this one
to smile enigmatically at that stranger down the bar,
the one with the hot mouth and wire rim glasses.
I will say how happy I am
to be able to play
Born in the U.S.A. on the jukebox
and live in a country where I am still free to read
Mein Kampf or the *Sayings of Chairman Mao*
in plain sight on the Brighton BMT.
Then I will say how happy I am
to have outgrown dramas and drama queens,
I will say that life is a beautiful dream

containing times of unexpected trials and sorrows,
isn't it so?
I will tell you about the challenge of learning
to really listen to what someone else is saying
and to respond honestly from the center of my heart.
I want to tell you how happy I felt yesterday
driving through the projects,
when I saw girls jumping rope double dutch,
like I did when I was twelve.
I'm so happy, so thankful,
I have a brain inside my head
instead of a cash register or the
voice of my ex-mother-in-law.
I'm happy as a simultaneous orgasm,
happy as Watson was to be writing about Sherlock Holmes,
happy as Cheech and Chong,
happy as a red polka dot bikini
to be writing this happy poem.